Philippians

A BIBLE + DOODLE STUDY FOR STUDENTS

BY KRISTEN HE

BIBLE + doodle!

Philippians A Bible + Doodle Study for Students

Copyright © 2018 by Kristen He

Printed by CreateSpace, an Amazon.com Company

All rights reserved. No part of this publication, either text, artwork, or design may be reproduced in any form without written permission from Kristen He, except for brief quotations used in reviews.

Cover design: Dan and Kate Ng, Little Bird Studios, LLC
Cover images: Kari Denker

Scripture quotations are from the ESV® Bible (The Holy Bible, English Standard Version®), copyright © 2001 by Crossway, a publishing ministry of Good News Publishers. Used by permission. All rights reserved.

All images and doodles used by permission. Special thanks to the artists for their artwork.
    Educlips, www.edu-clips.com
    Freepik.
    Kari Denker
    Lapetitprune - Freepik

All fonts used by permission.

In loving memory of
James
Who, more than anyone I know,
lived the message of Philippians -
In pursuit of Christ and for the Gospel,
wholeheartedly and with great joy.

CONTENTS

The Guide (for Getting Started)..1

Introduction..7

Background..13

Chapter 1..19

Chapter 2..37

Chapter 3..51

Chapter 4..61

Wait! I'm Not Ready to Be Done with Philippians..75

What is the Gospel?..77

Doodle Library..79

the Guide

Getting Started with Bible + Doodle

Hello! I'm glad you're here.

And I'm glad you picked up my book. I wrote this for you - and for kids like you. I expect that you're past the Bible storybook stage of life and are looking to learn more about the Bible. You're old enough to read, but you sometimes find that reading the Bible on your own creates questions and confusion. That's where this Bible study can help.

Bible...Study?

How are you feeling right now? Excited? Nervous? Does the idea of studying the Bible make you want to run and hide...or take a nap? Bible study doesn't have to be boring, scary, or overly difficult. It takes work, but it is incredibly rewarding.

Like miners who dig deep beneath the surface in search of treasure, we will be digging deep to mine out truth that has the power to renew our minds, transform our hearts, and give us life. Are you in?

This Bible Study is Different

In this Bible study, you're going to read the Bible and record (and doodle!) what you learn. We'll walk through the meaning together, often by comparing what we read with other parts of the Bible. That can be the challenging part because you're working to see how it all fits together. But along the way you'll have lots of opportunities to express your creativity and journal your thoughts.

After we understand the meaning, you do the rewarding part of listening to God through His Word and the Holy Spirit, figuring out how what you have learned works into your heart and life.

But what if I don't draw?

I happen to believe that if you can add doodles or simple art to what you're learning, you'll remember it longer, so I will always encourage your creative side. Just remember - your Bible study notebook is a record of your learning first, a collection of doodles and art second.

Start simply. Your style develops over time.

Throughout our study I'll show you lots of examples that you can copy or use as a springboard for your own creative ideas. And you can browse all the doodles in one place, in the Doodle Library at the back of the book for more inspiration. Whatever you do, don't let frustration take over. Enjoy the process and learn as you go. Let your notebook be a reflection of your style, and let it be a place where your own style develops too. You will shine!

Recommended tools

*A Bible - make sure it's a Bible and not a Bible storybook. There are even free Bible apps if that's your preference.
*Pencil/pens/markers/colored pencils
*Notebook
   ~Enjoy **drawing**? Use a sketch book with blank pages
   ~Enjoy **writing**, making lists, and bullet points? Use a notebook with lined paper
*Fun extras like washi tape, gel pens, stickers, and sticky notes can help you personalize your notebook, but aren't essential.
*A friendly, knowledgeable adult - also not required, but if you get stuck or have questions s/he can help you.

Get into a Habit

Each day, you'll start by finding a quiet place where you can pray, read, think, doodle, and learn. Do as much as you can, or as much as you have time for that day. Each item is marked with a box that you can check off as you go. Do as much as you can in each section, but know that you are not required to complete every check box. You should not feel pressured, but you should feel challenged and stretched to grow. Then the next day, simply pick up where you left off.

Let's Get Started!

Here are your first two checkboxes.

☐ Read the Introduction to Philippians (pages 7-11). This will give you an overview, telling you what Philippians is about. The Introduction will also give you a sneak peak into how God might use this study in your life, so no skipping past it!

☐ Read and complete the Background section in your notebook (pages 13-16). Yes, it's another thing to check off before you even begin to read and study Philippians, but it's essential. So again, no skipping allowed.

Dig in.
Enjoy the Process.
Grow, Change, and Become.
It's Going to Be Good.

INTRODUCTION

The book of Philippians is one of Christianity's most loved books. Though it is only 4 chapters long, or just over 2 pages in most people's Bibles, people are constantly quoting verses from this book. Spend time among Christians and you will hear things like

*He who began a good work will bring it to completion
*At the name of Jesus every knee will bow
*Do everything without grumbling
*Rejoice in the Lord always
*The peace of God that surpasses all understanding
*I can do all things through Christ who strengthens me

Have you heard any of these verses before? It's amazing how many verses are quoted from Philippians, considering that the whole book is only 104 verses long. Yet more amazing than how often we quote this book are the circumstances surrounding its writing.

Philippians is one of the Apostle Paul's prison **epistles**, written while Paul was under house arrest. Paul was chained to a guard for over two years, waiting for a trial to determine whether he would live or die, all because he would not stop preaching that Jesus Christ is Lord and Savior. To add insult to injury, he had to pay for his imprisonment! (see Acts 28:30-32)

An epistle is a letter written by an apostle or early church leader, including Paul, Peter, James, and John. There are 21 epistles in the New Testament.

If you got a letter from someone in those circumstances, you might expect to hear "Poor me, the prison rats are my only friends." "Gee, I'm getting skinny from the stale bread and water diet over here!" And, "Any news of when I might get out?" Or maybe even a question of "Why me?"

Yet you hear none of that in Paul's letter. What do you hear instead?

JOY.

Unstoppable, overflowing, contagious joy. Paul is in prison, chained to a stinky Roman guard, and he's rejoicing. Why? Or more importantly, how?

If you've read the book of Acts, you might remember that Paul getting imprisoned wasn't a one time fluke. You may also remember that when Paul became a Christian, God said that Paul was His chosen instrument to spread the Gospel even among kings (!) - but at the same time God would show Paul how much he would suffer for His name (Acts 9:15-16).

And God did not exaggerate.

Before Paul was imprisoned this time, he had been falsely accused and arrested (Acts 21:27-36). He was so hated by unbelievers that his enemies vowed they wouldn't eat until they killed him! He waited *years* before anyone would listen to his side of the story! Then, on the way to his trial, he went weeks without food, was shipwrecked, was nearly killed by a guard, was bitten by a poisonous snake, and was undoubtedly troubled and inconvenienced in countless other ways. (Acts 27-28)

8

This is the same man who writes, "Rejoice, again I say rejoice." The word "joy" (or some variation of it) occurs in Philippians 16 times - that's an average of 4 times per chapter!

rejoice

Again, WHY is Paul rejoicing? *How* is Paul rejoicing?

Quite simply, he's found something better. Better than a comfortable, easy, snake-free life. More valuable than freedom, good health, and decent meals three times a day. Of infinitely more value to him even than his own life.

What on earth is that?

CHRIST.

Christ is better. Christ is more. Christ is infinitely more worthy and valuable to Paul than even his own life.

That's how Paul can rejoice. He knows he is imprisoned because of Christ, on behalf of Christ and the gospel, and so he is filled with joy. He knows that all his sufferings are leading him to know Christ more, to understand more of who Christ is, and to experience more of God's presence in his life.

What a testimony of the power of God! Surely there is no greater way to show the world the glory of Christ than in the midst of suffering - when you have lost everything, including your own freedom - to be able to say, "I count my own life as worth nothing, if only I can know who Jesus is" (Philippians 3:8).

What about you, dear friend? Are Jesus Christ and the Gospel that valuable to you? Would you stick by Jesus if it meant you lost friends, lost a meal, were in a car wreck, lived daily under the threat of death, and lost your freedom?

Maybe you are reading this and you're not even sure who Jesus is. That's okay. This study will show you who Jesus is and will also explain the good news of the Gospel. Through this study you can come to know something (Someone) of infinitely more worth than whatever else you have been relying on for joy, strength, and security up to this point in your life. This study is for you.

Or maybe you have been a Christian a long time, but you struggle to be happy, much less joyful. There's just not that much in your life that brings joy right now. This study is for you, too.

Maybe, you really want to follow God, but when the hard choices come between obeying Christ or keeping your friends, you choose your friends. That's okay too. But its only "okay" if you don't stay there. I hope you'll allow Paul to show you a better way.

I hope that no matter where you are today in your walk with God that this study excites you. I hope you are ready to hear Paul's words scribbled from a jail cell and hand-carried across miles of cobbled roads from Rome to Philippi. I hope you are ready to study this ancient letter, written to encourage persecuted Christians who didn't grow up in Christian families knowing all about Jesus and going to church. But most of all, I hope you are ready for more - more of God's Word to you, more prayers, more questions, more seeking, and more finding.

Because Christ is better.

> ## ONE MORE THING...
>
> Throughout the study you will see boxes like this one. Along the way I'll be sharing stories from persecuted Christians around the world. Most have already died, though some are still alive today. All are known for following the example of Christ and the apostle Paul,
>
> > "for they loved not their own lives, even unto death." (Revelation 12:11)
>
> May their words and their faith inspire you to follow Jesus with utter abandon.

BACKGROUND

☐ Open your notebook to a fresh, clean page. Make a title page for your study, labeling it Philippians. You can box it in, draw a scroll around it, or doodle something else creative.

-PHILIPPIANS-

To start our study, we will first look at the background. Unfortunately, a lot of people want to skip this step because they think, maybe, that it is boring or unimportant. Sadly, if you're only willing to read the Bible but are never willing to *study*, your understanding is always going to be limited. So don't be one of those people who skips this part.

We want to make sure we are understanding the context of the book by studying the author, the audience, and the setting. Understanding the context helps us understand the meaning.

For example, imagine this conversation.
Me: Do you want tea?
You: No, thanks.

If you are from the West, you will interpret that conversation in a very straightforward way. You told me you don't want tea, and I won't give you any.

Now imagine that we are Asian. You say, "No, thanks," but I give you tea! Why? Because in the East, saying "no" when you mean "yes" is being polite. Saying "yes" is actually pushy and rude. So you *say* "no," but I know you *mean* "yes," and so I pour the tea. What?!

This is a very simple example, but it illustrates that context is really (really) important to understanding the meaning. Just imagine how much you would need to learn to avoid misunderstandings and truly understand someone from another culture!

In the same way, the book of Philippians was written in a specific culture, at a specific time. We might not think about that because we have our own copy of an English Bible, making it easy to forget that this is an ancient book written in Greek. But it doesn't make the importance of context any less true.

What did God's Word to the Philippians mean to the Philippians? Looking at the background will help us answer that question. And if we can answer that question, then we will know how God is speaking to each of us in the time and place we find ourselves today.

☐ Open your notebook to a new page. You're going to make entries for the author, the audience, and the location. You can make three large boxes all on the same page. Or, if you really enjoy history and background, you can devote an entire page to each of these things.

-authOR-

☐ We have already noted that the Apostle Paul is the author of Philippians (Philippians 1:1). In your notebook, draw a picture of the Apostle Paul. If you read Philippians 1:12-14 you will notice that Paul is imprisoned, so you might want to draw him with chains.

HELP! - In the back, on pages 80-81 you can find a step by step tutorial on how to draw "bowling pin style" Paul.

☐ What do you know about the Apostle Paul? You already know he wrote Philippians, so write that down. Then take some time to read about him, adding what you learn to your list. We will add more as we learn more, so be sure to leave extra space.

*Paul's violent and malicious pre-Christian days, when he was known as Saul. (Acts 7:54-60, Acts 8:1-3)

*Paul's dramatic conversion to Christianity (Acts 9:1-22)

*The many persecutions Paul endured as he worked to spread the gospel (2 Corinthians 11:23-28)

"Saul, why are you persecuting me?"

-audience-

Paul writes in Philippians 1:1 "to all the saints in Christ Jesus who are in Philippi." As you read, you will see how much Paul truly loved these believers. He was the first person to share Christ with them, and that was undoubtedly a special bond. The Philippians loved Paul too. While he was in prison, they prayed for him and sent him money to provide for his daily needs.

☐ Read about the first Philippian believers in Acts 16:9-40. Write down what you learn about Lydia, the slave girl, and the jailer in your notebook.

PURPLE FABRIC for Sale

-SETTING-

The city of Philippi was a Roman colony in Macedonia (which is now Greece). Philippi was a major city on the Roman highway known as the Via Egnatia. Philippi was built to model Rome and looked so similar that it was known as "Little Rome." The people of Philippi were Roman citizens who dressed like Romans, spoke Latin like educated Romans (instead of Greek), and enjoyed many other special privileges. They did not have to pay taxes and were excused from military duty. As citizens of Rome, the Philippians would have been expected to worship according to the imperial cult, which meant that Caesar and his family members were to be worshipped as gods. At the time Paul wrote Philippians, people could be killed for saying Jesus (not Caesar) is Lord![1]

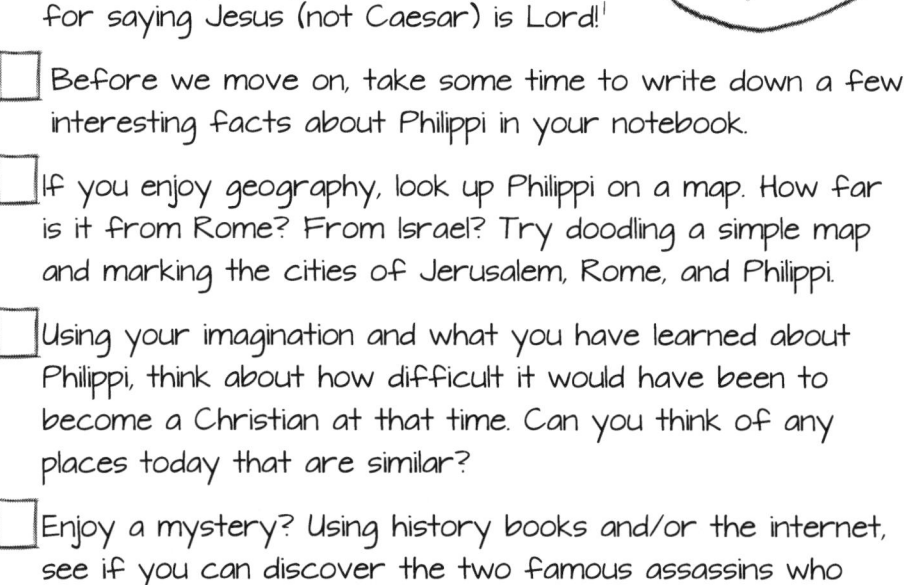

- ☐ Before we move on, take some time to write down a few interesting facts about Philippi in your notebook.

- ☐ If you enjoy geography, look up Philippi on a map. How far is it from Rome? From Israel? Try doodling a simple map and marking the cities of Jerusalem, Rome, and Philippi.

- ☐ Using your imagination and what you have learned about Philippi, think about how difficult it would have been to become a Christian at that time. Can you think of any places today that are similar?

- ☐ Enjoy a mystery? Using history books and/or the internet, see if you can discover the two famous assassins who were murdered in Philippi.

> ## John Chrysostom
>
> a church leader who was unafraid to unapologetically preach the word of God, was kidnapped by the Roman government and taken to Constantinople, unable to return home. At one point, he was told to renounce his faith and cease from preaching, or face the consequences. John would not. This, instead, was his response.
>
> If the empress wishes to banish me, let her do so; "the earth is the Lord's." If she wants to have me sawn asunder, I will have Isaiah as an example. If she wants to have me drowned in the ocean, I will think of Jonah. If I am to be thrown in the fire, the three men in the furnace suffered the same. If cast before wild beasts, I remember Daniel in the lion's den. If she wants to have me stoned, I have before me Stephen, the first martyr. If she demands my head, let her do so; John the Baptist shines before me. Naked I came from my mother's womb, naked shall I leave this world. Paul reminds me, "If I still pleased men, I would not be a servant of Christ."
>
> Eventually John was exiled, banished to live on the shores of the Black Sea where he died in 407, an enemy of the empire, a victorious overcomer in the Kingdom of God.[2]

Chapter 1

☐ Read the book of Philippians. I know, this is a pretty big ask right at the very beginning, but you can do it! Remember, it's probably less than 3 pages in your Bible. As you read, pay attention for any repeated words Paul uses, and try to get a general feel for why Paul is writing.

(If you *really* don't want to read, listen to someone read to you using Biblegateway.com or a similar website or app as you follow along. It will take less than 15 minutes to listen to the whole letter!)

Philippians 1:1-2

☐ Begin your time in prayer. Ask God to teach you wonderful truths from His Word.

☐ Read Philippians 1:1-2. This letter was written during the Roman Empire, around 61 A.D, so you will notice a very specific way that letters began - first who the letter is from, then who the letter is to.

☐ Open your notebook to a new page. Label it Philippians 1:1-2. (This can be fairly small, at the top of the page.)

☐ Who is writing the letter? If you completed the "Background" section, you know that Paul is the author. Yet here we see that Timothy is with him. Doodle Timothy and write down what you learn about him from these verses around your doodle.
  *Philippians 1:1
  *1 Timothy 1:2
  *2 Timothy 1:2-5

Philippians 1:1-2

☐ How does Paul describe himself in this passage? In almost every other epistle, Paul describes himself as an apostle of Jesus Christ. This time, however, he doesn't. Some Bible translations use the word "servants" while others say "bondservants." Interestingly, the original word in Greek can be translated "slave," which is even lower than a servant.

As pastor Steven Lawson explains, "A slave actually belonged to his master like a piece of property. He did not have a life of his own. Further, a slave did not own anything. He was entirely dependent upon his master to meet all his needs. Neither could he travel anywhere without his master's consent. His entire life existed to please his owner."[3]

☐ I love thinking about Paul in prison with such a faith-filled perspective that he sees God as his Master, not the guard he's chained to! Why do you think Paul described himself as God's slave? What similarities are there between a slave and a disciple? (See Mark 8:34-35.) Is this how you see yourself when you think about being a Christian? Journal your thoughts.

☐ Reread Philippians 1:2. Notice the two blessings Paul uses to greet the Philippians. Grace and peace are two very common words in the Bible and among Christians. (Sometimes you even hear people say we can't eat until we "say grace.") But do you know what they mean?

☐ Look up the words grace and peace in the dictionary, being careful to choose the definition(s) you think best fit Paul's meaning here.

PHILIPPIANS 1:1-2

☐ In your notebook, write out the words "grace" and "peace." Under (or around) the words, add what you learn about their meanings.

grace

AND

PEACE

Want to go deeper? Throughout the study there will be opportunities for deeper study. They will be marked with an arrow, like this one.

➡️

➡️ **Going Deeper:** Grace is a word that occurs repeatedly in the Bible, over 170 times in the New Testament alone.[4] It is difficult to define because no one word in English captures the full meaning. Read some or all of these verses on grace, adding what you learn to your journal page.

*John 1:14
*John 1:16
*Acts 4:33
*Ephesians 2:8-9
*Romans 11:5-6
*1 Corinthians 15:10
*2 Corinthians 4:15
*Titus 2:11

Philippians 1:3-11

☐ Begin your time in prayer. Ask God to speak to you through His Word. Ask God to help you understand who He is so that you will follow Him more closely. Thank Him for the time you have to read and study the Bible.

☐ Read Philippians 1:3-11. Notice how Paul feels towards the Philippians and some of the things he prays for them.

☐ Open your notebook to a new page. Label it Philippians 1:3-11.

☐ In your notebook you are going to make a chart like this one. You might want to turn your notebook sideways so that the chart can fill across the page. (Don't box things in until you finish writing.)

how Paul felt	WHY?	how Paul prayed
*		*
*		*
*		*
*		*

☐ Reread verses 3-11 to complete the chart. Look at verses 3, 4, 7, and 8 for the "how Paul felt" side. For example, in verse 4 he says "I always pray with joy," so you can write "joyful."

PHiLiPPiaNS 1:3-11

☐ For the "how Paul prayed" side of the chart you want to write down what he was praying for the Philippians (See verses 9-11). He is praying several things, and Paul tends to get long-winded when he prays. You don't need to write it out word for word; you can summarize it or write short phrases.

☐ Last, we come to the "why" part of the chart. It's the "why" that connects Paul's feelings and his prayers. Why did he feel the way he felt towards the Philippians? (See verses 5 and 7.) Add his reasons why to your chart.

☐ Now take a look at your journal page. What do you notice? You might notice how much Paul truly loves the Philippians. He sounds so emotional it is almost embarrassing, right? But I love why he feels that way - because they were his coworkers, his partners in spreading the Gospel. Paul might have been the one imprisoned, but they were all facing opposition and persecution for being Christians. Like Paul, these believers experienced God's grace in their lives in spite of opposition. This united them with a bond unique to believers.

☐ What do you notice about Paul's prayer for the Philippians? Is it focused on temporal things or eternal things? Focused on self or on others? With an attitude of gratitude or entitlement? Do you think Paul is praying according to God's will?

Philippians 1:3-11

☐ Before we leave this section, take some time to journal your thoughts based on the chart and your observations. Think through, journal, and pray about one or more of these questions. Ask God to teach you by His Spirit.

*Do you have Christian friends that you feel close to like Paul did? Do you and your friends support each other? Are you helping each other grow in your faith? Do you help carry their burdens? If you do not have this kind of Christian friend, have you asked God to give you one?

*Sometimes other believers are difficult to love. If there is another Christian you find hard to love, ask God to change your heart so that you can see His grace at work in their life (verse 7). When you can see others in process towards Christ-likeness (just like you!) you may find them easier to love. You can be patient with them, knowing that God is faithful to finish what he starts! (verse 6)

*How is Paul's prayer a model for what you can pray for yourself and others? Are you praying for others? Are you thankful for others?

Have you expressed thanks to God lately? Or do you think when blessings come it's "God's job" - that He owes you? If you're an entitled person, you won't be a grateful person. May God help us to see that we deserve nothing but judgment, and every good gift we have comes from Him.
~Tony Merida

Philippians 1:3-11

Going Deeper: In verse 9, Paul prays that their love would grow in knowledge and discernment. In the world today many people say that if you are loving you are "tolerant" of others, which usually means you are seen as hateful if you don't accept others' sinful choices. The Bible teaches, however, that love and truth go together.

You cannot love someone if you are unwilling to share the truth with them. You may have affection, you may be nice, but you are *not* loving. You will decide what to say based on how you feel. You won't say hard things because you fear what others will think. Your love is lacking knowledge and discernment.

At the same time, we can be incredibly unloving in the name of being right which is not Christ-like either. We might believe all the right things and even be able to quote the Bible, but we express those truths in ways that are full of our own pride. We are happy to speak out, even when it hurts others without building them up. Our knowledge and discernment lack love.

Remember that Satan, the world, and our flesh will always seek to divide what God has joined together. As we grow in our faith, we can avoid one extreme or the other.

For an example, read about the churches in Revelation. The church in Ephesus could discern false teachers yet lacked love (Revelation 2:1-5). On the other hand, the church in Thyatira had love but lacked knowledge, following false teaching (Revelation 2:18-23). Both were judged by God for what they lacked.[5]

Philippians 1:12-18

☐ Begin your time in prayer. Ask that God would reveal more of who He is to you as you study His Word. Pray that He would remove any sin, distraction, or obstacle in your life that keeps you from following Him wholeheartedly.

☐ Before you study Philippians today, first read the story of Paul preaching the Gospel in Thessalonica and Berea in Acts 17:1-15. As you read, pay close attention to the different reactions people have to Paul preaching. Using what you learn from the story, imagine what it must have been like to preach Christianity in the Roman empire in Paul's day! Notice the violently angry response from people who do not believe Paul's message about Jesus.

Just 30 or so years prior to Paul writing Philippians, the Jews had Jesus condemned and put to death, hoping to put an end to Christianity. Unfortunately, Christ's death and resurrection had the completely opposite effect. Within hours of the Holy Spirit being given to Christians, thousands were converted (Acts 2:41). In the days and months that followed, thousands more would trust Christ as their Savior (Acts 4:4, 5:14).

As the Gospel went out from Jerusalem, the Church faced opposition not only from the Jews but now also from unbelievers who worshipped idols and false gods. Believers were consistently thrown in prison in an effort to silence them. But the gospel continued to be proclaimed and God's church continued to grow.

Philippians 1:12-18

And so it is this time with Paul. He is imprisoned because of preaching the gospel, after being falsely accused, without a fair hearing or a trial. When he goes to trial, Caesar may decide he should be executed for his "crime."

☐ Read Philippians 1:12-18, paying close attention to Paul's attitude towards his imprisonment.

☐ Open your notebook to a new page and label it Philippians 1:12-18.

☐ In your notebook use doodles, a diagram, or even a simple list to summarize this passage. First look at the **obstacles** Paul was facing. His imprisonment, yes, and what else?

PROCLAIM — without fear

Next be sure to record the **outcomes** of Paul's imprisonment. Sure, Paul could have complained about how he wasn't able to preach, travel, or pastor churches the way he wanted. But what did he focus on instead? What is happening as a result of Paul's imprisonment? (See verses 13-14.)

gospel

Finally, what is the **end result**? Look especially at verses 12 and 18. Did Paul's imprisonment accomplish what his enemies hoped? Could prison silence Paul or keep the gospel from going out to others?

❓ What does it mean when Paul says "some preach Christ from envy and rivalry" (verse 15)? Though we can't know for sure, it seems that with Paul in prison some other pastors saw Paul's absence as a chance to build up their own ministries. Perhaps they even bad-mouthed Paul in order to get more people to attend *their* church instead of his. Crazy, but true.

Philippians 1:12-18

☐ Take some time to reflect on this passage (using your journal page to help). What do you think Paul believed about God that allowed him to rejoice during imprisonment? What was Paul depending on for his joy and happiness? (Or, was there anything Paul did not need in order to be happy?)

☐ What about you? What do you feel like you need in order to be happy? Do you feel like you *could* be really happy, but that God is holding out on you? You *could* rejoice, but God's just not answering your prayers? These are tough questions, but so worth taking the time to answer!

Journal your thoughts, and if you feel God is shining a light on a dark area of your heart, confess it to Him. Let Him know how you feel and where you struggle to have faith. Tell God about the things that bring you greater joy than a relationship with Him. There might be a lot of things, and that's okay. Ask Him to change you, that you could be the kind of Christian who has Christ as the source of their joy.

> You make known to me the path of life. In Your presence there is fullness of joy. At Your right hand are pleasures forevermore.
> ~Psalm 16:11

PHILIPPIANS 1:19-26

☐ Begin your time in prayer. Ask God to remove any distractions from you during this time so that you can focus on His Word. Praise God that through Jesus you can be in relationship with Him, that you are no longer His enemy. Thank Him for His love for you.

☐ Read Philippians 1:19-26. In these verses, Paul tells the Philippians about an internal debate going on in his heart.

☐ Label your notebook page Philippians 1:19-26.

As we know, Paul is in prison, and his life is on the line. Any day now, he may be called to testify before Caesar who could sentence him to death. He doesn't know how this will turn out. (And sadly, neither do we because the book of Acts, which recorded his imprisonment, ends abruptly without telling us what happened!)

LIFE? DEATH? Yet which I shall choose, I cannot tell....

☐ In your journal draw a picture of the Apostle Paul. On each side of Paul draw large thought bubbles - one labeled "life" and the other "death." Summarize Paul's thoughts on life in the body (on one side) versus death ("departing") on the other side. (See verses 21, 22, 24-26 for his arguments to keep on living. See verses 21 and 23 for why he is in favor of death..)

29

PHILIPPIANS 1:19-26

As you might expect from anyone facing the possibility of death, Paul starts to sound a little...shall we say...morbid. He doesn't necessarily want to die, yet he knows he might. Through eyes of faith, Paul realizes death is actually a good thing for the believer. Paul is living for Christ now, and he knows that when he dies, he gets even more of Christ, because he will be in God's presence forever.

☐ Read Philippians 1:21, one of Paul's most well known (and inspiring) expressions of faith. Open to a new page in your notebook and write out the verse. Underneath, write out your own version, filling in the blanks.

For me, to live is _____ and to die is _____ .

Maybe, if you're honest, you might write something like

For me, to live is good grades, and to die is an F.
Or
For me, to live is winning in sports, and to die is losing (or not being picked for the team).
Or
For me, to live is having the right friends, and to die is being rejected by them.

❗ Okay, now seriously, now is **not** the time for what I call a "Sunday school answer." You know what I mean - it sounds very good but is not very honest. Every one of us - even the most amazing Christian you know - has things we live for that are not Christ. If you feel bad about what you write, you can tear it out of your notebook later, but now is the time to be really (really!) super honest with yourself.

PHILIPPIANS 1:19-26

So what is it that you're living for? Where do you spend the most time, attention, or money? What part of your life - if you lost it - would make you feel like life is not worth living? Take some time to really ponder this question, filling in your version of verse 21 in your notebook. Then move on to the next part.

☐ In your notebook, take time to journal your thoughts. Do you notice that whatever filled your blank is temporary? What advantage is there for you if you could fill in your blank with something eternal? As you reflect, you may want to write out a prayer to God. Or maybe you want to talk to another Christian about how to enjoy and use the gifts God has given you (like intelligence or athletic ability) but not live for them. As Pastor Tony Merida says, "You want to spend your life on something that not only matters now but will also matter in a billion years."[6]

☐ Do you have the same confidence as Paul? Do you know without a doubt that you would be with Jesus if you died? If you have trusted in Christ as your Savior you can have assurance so that you do not live in fear of death. Jesus came to free us from fear and to give us eternal life with Him. Take time to read these verses to learn what the Bible teaches about heaven, death, and resurrection.

*Psalm 116:8
*John 11:21-27
*John 14:1-6
*1 Corinthians 15:51-55
*2 Corinthians 5:1-9
*1 John 5:13
*Revelation 21:1-4

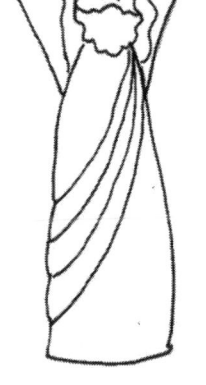

> **Nabeel Qureshi** was raised a devout Muslim, being able to read the entire Quran in Arabic by the time he was five years old. In college, he was befriended by a Christian and was confronted with the truth of the Gospel. When at last he became a Christian, he lost everything - his family, his friends, and his culture. This experience of loss was so painful that he actually wished God would kill him. Instead, God raised him up to defend the Christian faith before thousands. In reflection of the suffering he faced, he says,
>
> I will honestly say that my first year as a Christian was extremely difficult, without a doubt the most painful period of my life. Each and every day was a struggle, and I experienced depths of anguish I did not know possible.
>
> But I will also honestly say, looking back ten years later, that it was the most powerful and important time of my life. It shaped me, molded me, changed me into a disciple of Jesus. The Holy Spirit was my Comforter, His Word was my sustenance, and I would not give up that time for anything. The suffering is what made me into a true follower of Jesus. My life now, including my walk with God...is blissful, far more wonderful than I ever could have imagined when I was a Muslim.
>
> All suffering is worth it to follow Jesus. He is that amazing.[7]

PHILIPPIANS 1:27-30

☐ Begin your time in prayer. Think about the first time you heard the Gospel, if you can remember. Who shared the Gospel with you? Thank God for sending that person (or people) into your life to tell you about God, your sin, and forgiveness through Jesus. Then think about someone in your life who doesn't know Jesus. Pray for them now, asking God to draw them to Himself, that they would come to know Him and believe in Him as their Savior.

☐ Read Philippians 1:27-30. Paul has just finished talking about whether he lives or dies. In the end, he doesn't know if he will make it out of prison alive, so it's as if he's saying to the Philippians, "No matter what happens to me, you do this..." What is Paul encouraging the Philippians to do?

☐ Open your notebook to a new page. Label it Philippians 1:27-30. You'll notice in verse 27 that Paul tells the Philippians "Only let your manner of life be worthy of the Gospel..." Remember that Paul was writing to the Philippians, but this is God's Word to us too. Let's dive deep into this phrase, to grasp its meaning so that we can obey God's Word.

☐ At the top of your notebook page write "Worthy of the Gospel." Draw a simple balance like this one underneath the heading.

PHILIPPIANS 1:27-30

The word "worthy" is not one that we use very often, but it carries the idea of a scale or balance. What are we weighing on the scale? On one side, there is the gospel, the Good News of Jesus which is "weighty" - it has incomparable, eternal value.

☐ Label one side of your scale "The Gospel." To the side of it, write down words related to the gospel. (See also Ephesians 2:4-8 and Titus 3:4-7) You might write words like "gift" "salvation" "God's lovingkindness" "grace" and more.

> The Gospel is that Christ has suffered the full wrath of God for my sins. Jesus Christ traded places with me, living the perfect life I should have lived, and dying the death I had been condemned to die. He took my [sinful] record, died for it, and offers me His perfect record in return. He lived in my place, and died in my place, and then offered to me a gift.
> J.D. Greear[8]

☐ Now let's focus on the other side of the scale, what Paul calls "your manner of life." (Label your scale.) Paul is not talking about your manners, like whether you say "please" and "thank you." He means the way you conduct yourself, the way you live your life.

On our own, our manner of life would be described as sinful, selfish, empty, dead, in darkness, and more. But as children of God, we can now - through the power of the gospel and the Holy Spirit - live in a way that honors God and the gospel.

PHILIPPIANS 1:27-30

☐ Read verses 28-30. Paul tells the Philippians what he wants them to do and describes the kind of people he wants them to be. What does a life "worthy of the gospel" look like for Christians according to these verses? List them on your notebook page.

☐ At the bottom of your page, journal your thoughts. Does your life match the message of the gospel? Does your life reflect the love, forgiveness, and grace that you received when you received Christ? Where are you discrediting Christ and the gospel? Are you wavering in your faith? Are you willing to be seen as a Christian with one group of people but live like the world with another group? Are you frightened or intimidated into silence by non-Christians who oppose the gospel? Make these issues a matter of prayer, asking God to change you by His Spirit and His Word.

➡ **Going Deeper**: Read these verses for even more details from Paul on living in a worthy manner. What similarities do you notice?

*Ephesians 4:1-3
*Colossians 1:10-12

➡ **Going Deeper**: Read back through chapter 1, noting every time Paul mentions the gospel. He is absolutely consumed with the gospel! What else do you notice about Paul and the gospel? What do you learn?

Fadi Benosh

is a Christian youth pastor in the Muslim country of Iraq. One day, on his way home from helping another church plan after-school activities for children, he was kidnapped. He stopped to buy food at a fruit stand when six armed men wearing masks suddenly attacked him and shoved him into the trunk of a car. Fadi later reported,

"I felt my life stop in that moment. 'Jesus Christ! Jesus Christ!' I called from the trunk. I could not think of anything else."

Fadi was able to access his cell phone in the trunk. He called his home church in Bagdad. The church quickly organized prayer vigils for Fadi's safety and release.

The kidnappers called themselves *mujahideen*, Islam's fighters for Allah. They took Fadi and five others to a cave. When they learned that Fadi was a Christian, they quickly singled him out to die. One gunman repeated over and over, 'We must kill the Christian one, the one who doesn't believe in Allah. We have to kill him."

Inside the cave, Fadi continued to trust God. "I sensed that God was with me," he would later say.

After six days, he was let go, without any explanation or reason. Fadi believes that he was released because of the many prayers for him.[9]

Chapter 2

Philippians 2:1-4

- [ ] Begin your time in prayer. Thank God for this time, and ask that He would bless it, helping you to know Him more. Ask God to give you a humble, teachable spirit that wants to learn. Praise God for His Word that is powerful, true, and trustworthy.

- [ ] Read Philippians 2:1-4. In chapter 1, Paul encouraged the Philippians to stand together, working side by side for the gospel. In this passage, he encourages them to work and serve together in humility.

- [ ] Open your notebook to a fresh page, labeling it Philippians 2:1-4 at the top.

- [ ] In the middle of your page, write out an abbreviated version of verse 2, which is the main command Paul gives the Philippian believers. You can box it in or draw other doodles around it. Here's how I did it.

> **Same mind. Same love.**
> **—UNITED—**
> **One spirit. One purpose.**
> (verse 2)

- [ ] Now go back and reread verse 1, where Paul reminds the church of some of their many blessings. As you read, replace Paul's word "if" with "since." (Paul is not questioning whether they have those things. He is making a statement of fact. So you can read it as, "Since you have...")

37

Philippians 2:1-4

☐ Above the middle box where you drew the command, write down the blessings Paul mentions. You might want to draw arrows from the blessings towards the command.

I don't know about you, but I love how Paul first reminds the Philippians of what they have - encouragement, love, comfort, and more - and *then* tells them what to do. This should encourage us that God doesn't make unreasonable demands on His children. He first blesses us, and then asks us to obey.

☐ To finish, read verses 3-4. Think of these verses as Paul's way of filling in the details, giving several practical commands for how to be united (which he already commanded in verse 2).

☐ Below your command box, you're going to make two lists. Label one "DO" and the other "DON'T." Reread verses 3 and 4, writing out all the commands Paul gives. For example, under DON'T you could write "do things from selfish ambition" (verse 3).

☐ Finally, look at your notebook page. What do you notice? What really stands out to you? What action do you consistently do out of "selfish ambition" - to get ahead, go first, or try to prove yourself? Is there a gift that God has given to you that makes you feel conceited - that is, to feel "an excessively favorable opinion" of yourself? When is it hard for you to put others' needs before your own? What do these commands mean as you grow up in a selfie culture? These are hard questions, but remember that God has given you everything you need to live this out. Pray, rely on Him, and obey.

Philippians 2:5-11

- [ ] Begin your time in prayer. Today's passage focuses on Jesus Christ. Praise God for sending His Son to die in our place. Thank God for Jesus who made the way for us to know Him. Ask God to use this passage to open your eyes, to see Jesus more clearly.

- [ ] Read Philippians 2:5-11. Paul is quoting a hymn or creed from the early church in order to teach the Philippians some really important truths about Jesus and humility.

    Remember that in the verses leading up to this, Paul just commanded the Philippians to work together, not exalting themselves, and to be unified for the sake of the gospel. How can they do that? Through humility. Who will be their example? Jesus.

- [ ] Open your notebook to a new page and label it Philippians 2:5-11 at the top. This passage is a deep well of truth you can drink deeply from your whole life. Entire books have been written on just these 6 verses! I encourage you to dig in and take it slowly, verse by verse.

- [ ] Begin by defining humility. What does it mean to be humble? You can discuss it with others, look it up in the dictionary, or even make a list of what humility is *not*. Write down your ideas. Once you get a good idea of the meaning, move on to the next part.

> The Greeks did not even have a word for humility, because it was considered of such a low value. The concept was entirely foreign to the Greeks and utterly abhorrent to the Romans.[10]

Philippians 2:5-11

In these verses, Paul is encouraging the Philippians to have a mindset of humility, just like Jesus did. Without humility, we are proud, self-absorbed, self-serving people. But Paul wants the Philippians (and us!) to be about Christ and the gospel. Yet how can I live for Christ or sacrifice for the gospel if I am the most important thing in my life? The answer, of course, is that I can't. Only by looking to Christ - allowing Him to expose our pride, allowing Him to show us how small we truly are - can we live to bring glory to God and not ourselves.

Let this mind be in you
humility
which is yours in Christ Jesus

☐ Doodle a picture of Jesus. Around the doodle write down everything Jesus did to humble himself based on this passage.

In the pages that follow, there are notes on these verses if you want to go deeper or understand the passage more. Go slowly and think deeply! Remember to add your own thoughts to your notebook as you study.

*who, though he was in the form of God - This does not mean that Jesus only *appeared* to be God. Paul wrote Philippians in Greek, and the Greek word "form" (*morphe*) means the inner nature, so Paul is saying "though his very essence was God..." Read John 1:1-5, Colossians 1:15-20, and Hebrews 1:1-3 which all testify to Jesus' divine nature.

Philippians 2:5-11

(Also notice that all of these passages speak about Jesus as Creator. Creator - *not* created, as many false religions believe.)

did not count equality with God something to be grasped, but emptied Himself - one of my family's favorite movies is *The Emperor's New Groove* which tells the story of a very bratty emperor, Kuzco. Surrounded by servants, he uses his status as king to be entirely self-serving. He relishes his ability to boss people around, and he lives to soak up all the praise from his subjects. The story centers on his plans to destroy an entire village in order to get what he wants - a swimming pool! Though the movie is quite funny, Kuzco is also entirely what we might expect from a king, isn't he?

In Jesus, though, we see the exact opposite. As King of the universe from eternity past, no one has ever had a greater kingdom or one that has lasted as long. No earthly king has ever had angels as subjects, or the power to command the stars! As King, Jesus could have remained in heaven, holding on to His status as God, forever enjoying all the pleasures, rights, and privileges as God and King. Instead, He gave up everything (which is the meaning of "emptied Himself"). No more worship. No more heavenly comforts. No longer in the presence of God the Father. Why? In order to give, to bring us salvation.

Philippians 2:5-11

In contrast, we fight and squabble and grasp for every little thing, as if we imagine ourselves to be royalty. If only everyone could remember how great we are! "That last cookie was MINE!" "That is MY seat!" "Get out of MY way!" How quick we are to snatch what is ours, how slow to offer freely.

Can you see how a mindset of humility can lead to unity? How easy do you think it would be to get along with others if instead of fighting for your rights, you gave up what you wanted in order to give to others? Hmm....

*by taking the form of a servant - Just as earthly kings have multitudes of servants to meet their every need, so it would have been appropriate if Jesus had come to earth and had us serve Him. He is King, after all! Yet He did not come to have us meet His needs. He came to meet *our* greatest need - our need for a Savior. See Mark 10:45.

*He humbled himself by becoming obedient to death, even death on a cross - Death by crucifixion is one of the most violent, cruel, and tortuous means of execution developed by fallen mankind in the history of the world. The pain of the cross was so unbearable that a word had to be invented to describe it: "excruciating" (which in Latin means "from the cross"). Romans saw crucifixion as so horrible that people shouldn't even think or speak about it.[ii] Read Isaiah 53 or Mark 15:1-39 and note the many humiliations Jesus endured to pay for our sin.

PHILIPPIANS 2:5-11

*Therefore God has exalted him...so that at the name of Jesus every knee should bow...and every tongue confess that Jesus Christ is Lord - after Jesus' resurrection, he not only ascended to heaven, but was raised to the right hand of God (Acts 2:32-33). He has supreme authority and power. And one day, every single created being will bow down in submission, and will openly declare His authority (see Isaiah 45:22-23).

LORD of ALL

*in heaven, and on earth, and under the earth - No one will be excused from recognizing Jesus as Lord. Not angels in heaven, nor people on earth, nor demons in hell.

*to the glory of God the Father - Jesus did not obey God the Father to win glory for Himself. His life, death, resurrection, and exaltation all bring glory to God.

☐ You made it through! Hopefully all that you learned made your effort worth it. Before we move on, you may want to take a final moment to reflect, journal, and pray.

-What one area of your life could you ask God to change so that you are more willing to give to others instead of get for yourself?

-How does Jesus' humility change your idea of who He is as God? Does it affect your worship of Him?

-Jesus is our example of humility. But He is not *only* an example. He is also Lord. Is He Lord in your life? Is there an area in your life where you are unwilling to obey God? Confess your sin to God, asking Him to change you.

43

PHILIPPIANS 2:12-16

- [ ] Begin your time in prayer. Spend some time praising God for who He is, but instead of saying, "Thank you, God, for being loving," or "I praise You, God, because You are loving," say, "God, You are loving" adding any thoughts you have about how God has shown His love to you. (This is just an example.) God is truth, all powerful, righteous and just, merciful, patient, and more! What will you praise Him for today? End your prayer by asking God to bless this time of study, to teach you by the Holy Spirit, and to make you the kind of Christian who wants to learn and grow in your faith.

- [ ] Read Philippians 2:12-16. You will notice Paul gives several commands and exhortations to the Philippians for how they should live as Christians. As you read, think about how these commands connect to Paul's teaching on humility in the previous verses.

- [ ] Open your journal to a new page and label it Philippians 2:12-16 at the top.

- [ ] Look again at verse 12. In most translations, this verse starts with "Therefore" or "Since then." These words act like a hinge, connecting the coming verses to the ones before it. So whenever you come across this word or phrase in your Bible, you should always ask yourself how it connects to the previous verses. (Or, as some like to say, "When you see the word 'therefore,' you should ask, "What is the therefore there for?")

PHILIPPIANS 2:12-16

As we think back on the previous verses, Paul seems to be telling the Philippians that because of Christ's example of humility, because one day we will bow down before Jesus Christ our Lord, we should be obedient. He writes, "as you have always obeyed..." (verse 12). A humble mindset will always show itself in obedience.[12] Proud people are disobedient people. Why? Because they believe their way is the best way, so they won't listen to anyone tell them what to do. In contrast, people who are humble trust God's Word to teach them. A humble person willingly bends his will and his desires to God (or to others in authority over him), listening to what God says, and then doing it. (Even when - or especially when - it hurts!)

GOD OPPOSES THE PROUD BUT GIVES GRACE TO THE humble

☐ So, as Paul has commanded us to be humble (verses 3, 5), let's note all the ways we, as children of God, should obey God based on this passage. In the center of your notebook page, draw yourself (or a stick person). Around your doodle, write down words and phrases that should describe our lives as children of God from the passage. For example, "obedience" (verse 12) and "no grumbling" (verse 14).

SHINING LIKE STARS IN THE SKY

Philippians 2:12-16

☐ Look at your notebook. What stands out to you? Is there a verse that really encourages you? What does it mean for you right now to be shining like a light in the world? Or, is there an area in your life where you could display more humility and obedience? (Maybe there is a particular person you struggle to be respectful to, or maybe it is a certain circumstance that always seems to bring out your pride?) Journal your thoughts.

❓ You may have noticed the tricky phrase, "work out your own salvation" in verse 12. Is Paul saying we can work to earn our salvation by doing good works? If so, he is contradicting the Bible's teaching that we are saved by grace alone through faith alone.

We can always trust the Bible to be consistent. So when we come across a passage that seems to contradict another passage, we must look closely to make sure we are understanding the meaning.

Looking closely at verse 12 we notice that Paul says work *out* your salvation. He never says work *for* your salvation. Read Ephesians 2:8-10 and Titus 3:4-8 which also teach that God saves us by His grace, and *then* we do good works.

> Since God has operated in, you can work out. God has already saved you within and has given you life. Now there is no other way but to let Him come out.
> -Watchman Nee-

> ## Polycarp,
> the pastor of the church in Smyrna, was arrested and carried before the proconsul. During his trial, the proconsul urged him to deny his faith. "Swear, and I will release you. Reproach Christ."
>
> Polycarp boldly answered, "Eighty and six years have I served Him, and He never once wronged me. How then shall I blaspheme my King, who has saved me?"
>
> At this, Polycarp was condemned to death and led to the marketplace where he was tied to the stake. Usually martyrs were nailed to the stake before being burned alive, but Polycarp assured them he would not move. It is reported that when the executioner lit the fire to burn him at the stake, the flames strangely arched above him, without touching him. When the executioner saw this, he was ordered to kill Polycarp with the sword.
>
> Polycarp died in 162, an enemy of the Jews and the Roman empire (under Marcus Aurelius Antoninus), yet a victor in heaven.[13]

PHILIPPIANS 2:17-30

☐ Begin your time in prayer. Reflect on God's mercy, which is His kindness, compassion, and blessing, especially to those who are undeserving. What evidence do you have of God's mercy in your life? Thank God for His mercies which are new with each and every day.

☐ Read Philippians 2:17-30. As you read think about how these three men (Paul, Timothy, and Epaphroditus) are living lives of humility and obedience to Christ.

☐ Open your notebook to your page on Paul (from the Background section). Reread verse 17 and add what you learn to your notebook.

Remember that Paul had been imprisoned in Philippi for sharing the gospel with the Philippians. After his release from jail, Paul didn't stop preaching, so the persecution did not stop either. When Paul says he's being poured out, surely he is expressing his willingness to sacrifice even his own life in order to see others believe in Jesus. He gives up comfort and security for the sake of Christ and the gospel. What is Paul's attitude towards his sacrifice?

the way back to Philippi

☐ Now turn to your page on Timothy, (from Chapter 1). Read Philippians 2:19-22 and add what you learn about Timothy to your notebook. Try your best to summarize Paul's description in your own words.

PHILIPPIANS 2:17-30

☐ Turn to a new page in your notebook and label it Philippians 2:17-30 at the top.

☐ Read Philippians 2:25-30 and Philippians 4:16-18. Draw a picture of Epaphroditus in your notebook, adding what you learn about him from these passages. It's interesting to think about a time when weeks or months would have passed before you could hear news about your friend's illness!

☐ Before we finish Philippians 2, return to your notebook page where you first defined humility. Now that you have studied the examples of Jesus, Paul, Timothy, and Epaphroditus what would you add to your definition? Has your definition of humility changed at all?

A huge part of humility is putting others' needs before our own. We may imagine ourselves living heroic Christian lives in prison or sick to the point of death for Christ and the gospel. Yet if we're honest, we are often unwilling to make tiny sacrifices in order to bless others. How hard it is to get off the screen in order to listen to someone else! What a challenge to get out of bed in order to bless my parents! How painful to give away a few dollars instead of spending it on myself!

God does ask us to give our very lives for Him, and for some that means we will be martyred or imprisoned. Yet He daily calls all of us to a lifestyle of small sacrifices so that others may know Him. Make it your prayer that you will follow Him wholeheartedly and sacrificially.

I WILL FOLLOW

> **Speratus** was brought before the Roman governor with other Christians for interrogation. Their crime? They refused to believe that the emperor was God. When the governor demanded that they "swear by the divine spirit of our lord the emperor" Speratus replied,
>
> "I do not recognize the empire of this world. Rather, I serve the God whom no one has seen nor can see with physical eyes...I recognize my Lord, who is Emperor over kings and the entire human race."
>
> The governor continued to interrogate the group of Christians, nearly pleading with them to abandon their "insanity" of believing in God.
>
> Finally, unable to persuade them, the governor offered them thirty days to think about their decision. Perhaps they would recant and change their minds. Maybe, after thinking about it, they would stop believing in Christianity and worship the emperor instead.
>
> However, rather than take the thirty days, Speratus and the others simply continued to declare "I am a Christian!"
>
> Seeing that they refused to be persuaded and would not return to "Roman ways," the governor ordered that they be executed. On July 17, 180 A.D., Speratus and the other believers with him were beheaded for the name of Christ.[4]

Chapter 3

Philippians 3:1-11

☐ Begin your time in prayer. Praise God for making a way for salvation through faith in Jesus. Thank Him that we are saved by His grace, not because of any good thing that we have done. Praise Him for accepting us because of all that Jesus did in his death, burial, and resurrection. Finally, ask God to guide your time of study by the Holy Spirit, that He would lead you to the truth.

☐ Read Philippians 3:1-11. As you read, notice the contrast Paul makes between "the dogs" and himself.

☐ Open your notebook to a fresh page and label it Philippians 3:1-11 at the top. In this passage, Paul is warning the Christians in Philippi about false teachers known as the Judaizers (though they are not called that here). The Jews are people who are descendants of Abraham. Everyone else is a Gentile. The Judaizers were Jewish converts to Christianity who taught that Gentiles could not be true Christians unless they first "became Jewish" by following the Old Testament Law (like the 10 Commandments and circumcision), *and* believing in Jesus. Paul condemns them for "putting confidence in the flesh." That is, the Judaizers were trying to find salvation in something *they* did (following the law), *not* by faith in Jesus alone.

51

PHILIPPIANS 3:1-11

☐ Turn your notebook so that your page is horizontal. Label one half "Confidence in the Flesh." Then list out all the things that Paul *could* put confidence in, if he were following the Judaizers' teaching. You will find quite a list in verses 4-6. And don't forget to chuckle here, Paul is being classic Paul, sarcastically exaggerating to make a point.

☐ After making your list, look at verses 7-8 where Paul says he "counts them" (or adds them up) to equal....what? Some translations say rubbish or garbage. The King James translates it "dung" which is getting pretty close to what Paul wrote in Greek (He actually uses a stronger, coarser word!) Needless to say, Paul did not think all that he had done (which was an impressive list by the Judaizer's standards) amounted to much. He quite literally equates all his human goodness to a big pile of poo.

CIRCUMCISED
JEWISH
TRIBE OF BENJAMIN
•
•
•
✝ •
―――――――
RUBBISH

WORSHIP BY THE SPIRIT OF GOD
GLORY IN CHRIST JESUS
GAIN CHRIST
FOUND IN HIM
NO RIGHTEOUSNESS OF MY OWN
•
•
•
✝
―――――――
SURPASSING WORTH

☐ Now label the other side of your page "No Confidence in the Flesh." List out all the things Paul has gained and how he describes his life in Christ. Start in verse 3, then skip down to verses 9-11.

In verse 8 Paul counts this list as "surpassing worth." Why? What makes this list so valuable? What made this righteousness different than the righteousness he earned?

PHILIPPIANS 3:1-11

What about you? Is there anything that you are trusting in for salvation? Maybe, like the Judaizers, you believe you are a Christian because you were born into a Christian family, or were baptized. You say you're a Christian because you are really sincere about your faith, or are good at following rules. To the contrary, Paul says that all that is absolute trash, unable to save us.

Our confidence for salvation must be in Christ alone, through faith alone, by grace alone.

Or maybe you know that nothing you do can save you, but... you feel like God approves of you more when you are reading your Bible, going to church, and praying regularly. Perhaps you're struggling to believe God's acceptance of you. This was a struggle I had for years after I had become a Christian. I knew God loved me - that's practically His job, right? - but did God *like* me? Did He approve of me? Didn't He like me more when I acted more like a Christian? Of course He did, right? If I was faithful to read my Bible and pray, God was surely happier with me, right? I felt awful if I skipped church, fought with my parents, or fell asleep during prayer. Surely God was disappointed in me too. Right?!

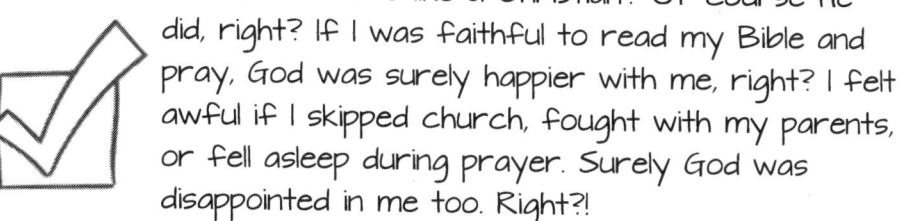

Thankfully, friends, I was *not* right. But it took studying and understanding a big word found in the Bible before I realized just how wrong I was.

The word?

JUSTIFICATION.

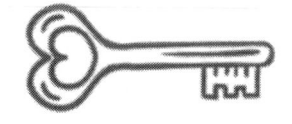

53

Philippians 3:1-11

Although Paul doesn't use the word here, he refers to it when he says he trusts in Christ to *receive* righteousness from God.

☐ To understand justification, imagine a report card where you are graded on honesty, kindness, and patience.[15] In this imaginary classroom, God is handing out the grades. For you and me, the Bible tells us that we got straight F's. Failing in every single category. (Isaiah 64:6) Imagine taking that report card home!

But God did not leave us there. He sent Jesus. When we trust Christ to save us, we are forgiven. It's as if all those bad grades were wiped away. (Psalm 103:12) What a relief!

But justification goes a step further. Justification means that God not only forgives us, but that He takes Jesus' record - a perfect report card of all A++'s, if you can imagine - and gives us that instead.

In the Bible, justification means that our sinful record is removed and that we receive - by the sheer grace of God - Jesus' perfect record instead.

So when we think about whether or not God approves of us, is there anyone God approves of more than Jesus? Definitely not. Is there anything you or I could do to improve on Jesus' record? Again, definitely not. Understanding justification means that we never have to wonder about God's approval of us again.

☐ Read Romans 5:1, Galatians 2:16, and 2 Corinthians 5:21. How are we justified? Can we earn it? Can we add to our righteousness? What would you say to a Christian who feels like God is disappointed in them?

PHILIPPIANS 3:1-11

Dressed in His Righteousness Alone

Faultless to stand before the throne

☐ Take time to journal your thoughts. How would you explain justification to someone else? Why is it important to understand? How can it change your relationship to God? Do you think it will change your willingness to obey God?

➡ **Going Deeper** - If you're not yet ready to leave this section, take some time to learn more about the Judaizers. It may seem easy for us to see that their teaching was false, but in the first century church it was a big problem. To understand why, you need to understand that God had spoken to the Jewish people, setting them apart from other nations by giving them the Law. One of the Law's requirements was circumcision.

Read Exodus 12:48 and Ezekiel 44:9. In the Old Testament, any non-Jewish person who wanted to worship with the Jews had to be circumcised.

Then came Jesus, the gospel, and the start of the Church. The gospel came first to the Jews (Romans 1:16). It's likely that years passed before the gospel was preached to the Gentiles (Acts 10:30-35), and when Gentiles believed in Jesus, the Church was utterly amazed. They were also pretty upset (Acts 11:1-18). How could the Gentiles be saved without first "becoming Jewish" (by circumcision)? Read Acts 15, where the church gathered together to debate this problem. Finally, read Paul's teaching to other churches on this issue in Titus 1:10-11 and Galatians 5:2-6

**ONE LORD
ONE FAITH
ONE BAPTISM
ONE GOD
and
FATHER of ALL**

❝ **Vibia Perpetua**
was an educated noblewoman from Carthage, North Africa. In 203, she was put under house arrest, and then jailed for her faith. During her imprisonment, her father repeatedly visited her in order to convince her to stop believing in Christianity. Although Perpetua was only 22, she refused to be persuaded, but held fast to her faith.

Soon after her imprisonment, she was brought before the governor. She could be released from prison, he said, if she would sacrifice to the emperor. Perpetua adamantly refused, declaring, "I won't! I am a Christian."

Perpetua returned to prison, to await the day of the gladiator games where she and other Christians would be thrown to wild beasts before a huge crowd in the amphitheater.

On the day of the games, the Christians were led to the amphitheater, proceeding cheerfully as if they were marching to heaven. Perpetua was calm and radiant. At first, she was thrown before a wild cow who tossed her body, tore her clothes, and gashed her open. She remained brave. Her last words were to fellow believers in the amphitheater.

"Stand firm in the faith! And all of you must love one another! Don't let our martyrdom be a stumbling block to you!"

At last when the crazed cow failed to kill her, a gladiator came forth and killed her with his sword.[16] ❞

PHILIPPIANS 3:12-21

☐ Begin your time in prayer. Today, base your prayer on Psalm 25:4-5. You can read the verses aloud as a prayer. Or, you can read a phrase, add your own thoughts and prayers, then go on to the next phrase. May this be your heart today as you study God's Word!

> Make me to know your ways,
> O Lord; teach me your paths.
> Lead me in your truth &
> teach me, for you are
> the God of my salvation;
> for you I wait all the day long.
> PSALM 25:4-5

☐ Read Philippians 3:12-21 as Paul describes his walk with God like a race towards a finish line. As you read, notice the contrast between Paul (and those imitating him) and the "enemies of the cross of Christ."

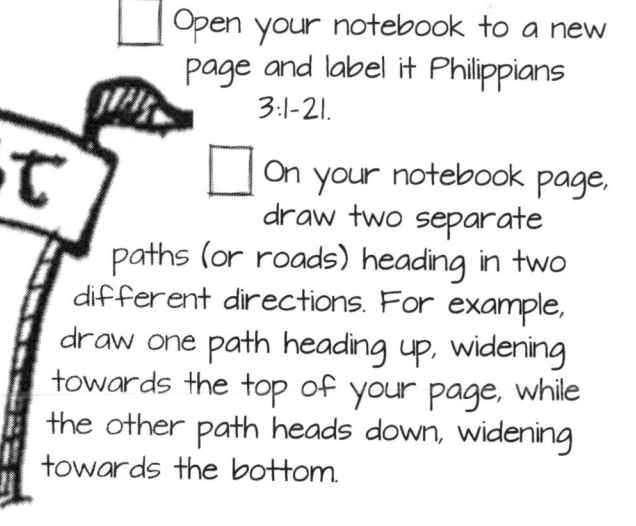

☐ Open your notebook to a new page and label it Philippians 3:1-21.

☐ On your notebook page, draw two separate paths (or roads) heading in two different directions. For example, draw one path heading up, widening towards the top of your page, while the other path heads down, widening towards the bottom.

Philippians 3:12-21

☐ On the first road, the one heading up, write down all the words and phrases you see that Paul uses to describe his pursuit of Christ. These are found in verses 12-16. For example, you could write down "forgetting the past," "pressing on," and "mature." Write down all you find. (Try to write down at least 5.)

☐ At the end of your road, draw a cloud or a starburst. Reread verses 20-21. Where is this road heading? Paul is looking towards heaven where he will be with Jesus, so you could write down words in the cloud that describe the destination.

☐ Reread verses 18-19 where Paul describes those on the opposite road. Write down all Paul says about them in these verses.

☐ At the end of this road, draw a scribble or explosion. What is the end for those who walk on this road?

☐ Read Jesus' teaching about two roads in Matthew 7:13-14. How is Paul's teaching similar to Jesus'?

☐ What about you? What road are you on? Are you running hard towards Jesus and Christlikeness? Do you discipline yourself, making time for prayer and Bible study? Are you fighting temptation? Or are you ambling along, doing whatever suits you in the moment, heading towards destruction? Are you wasting your life? If this is you, when will you commit to following Christ wholeheartedly? Why not today? Take some time to prayerfully consider these questions and journal your thoughts.

PHILIPPIANS 3:12-21

☐ In the previous section on Philippians 3:1-11 we studied justification. We have God's approval because He gave us His righteousness through Jesus. In that section, I asked you if believing in justification could influence your obedience to God. What do you think? If you believe you are already righteous before God, are you more willing to obey God or are you less willing to obey God?

Why work when you can sleep? ZZZZ

Over the course of history, many have feared that if people believe in justification they will become lazy and increasingly sinful, feeling they don't need to obey God. "God already sees me as righteous. Why should I live righteously? That means work for me. I'd rather just go on sinning and live life my way."

You can see from this passage, however, that Paul did not think this way. In the first part of chapter 3 he boldly proclaimed that he was trusting in Jesus for righteousness. Just a few verses later, he's talking about straining forward, pressing on, exerting all energy to follow Christ. Why? How is this possible?

PRESS ON...

HEAVEN BOUND

The key, I believe, is in verse 12 where Paul says "I press on to make it my own because Christ Jesus has made me His own." That is, Jesus had completely captivated Paul's heart. He was utterly transformed by the gospel. He grasped what amazing grace had been given to him. Now, out of love, gratitude, and devotion to Christ, Paul was doing everything he could to become more like Jesus. Not because he *had* to, but all because he *wanted* to.

☐ Journal what you're thinking and learning.

Nate Saint

was trained as a pilot with a deep desire to serve the Lord. In 1948, at the age of 25, he moved to Ecuador as a missionary pilot. He was instrumental in establishing a mission airbase in Ecuador, enabling missionaries to receive much needed supplies in the remote jungles.

However much he loved flying airplanes, though, Nate loved the Lord even more. His desire to go into all the world and spread the gospel was a burning desire in his heart. He longed to share the good news of Christ's salvation with the Auca tribe of Ecuador. The Aucas were warriors, infamous for their brutal killing sprees.

In 1955, Nate, together with four other missionaries, began to establish a relationship with the Aucas by dropping gifts from Nate's plane. They all knew it was incredibly risky, possibly endangering their lives. Yet they were utterly compelled by their love for Christ and their passion to share with the unreached.

In a letter home, Nate wrote,
"If God would grant us the vision, the word sacrifice would disappear from our lips and thoughts. We would hate the things that now seem so dear to us. Our lives would suddenly seem too short. We would despise time-robbing distractions and charge the enemy with all our energies in the name of Christ."

On January 8, 1956, Nate and the 4 other missionaries were speared to death by the Aucas. Miraculously, their martyrdom lead to saving faith of many Aucas, including six of the warriors who killed the missionaries.[17]

Chapter 4

Philippians 4:1-5

- [ ] Begin your time in prayer. Thank God for this time to study the Bible. Ask that He would give you a heart that loves His Word. Pray that you would listen to Him.

- [ ] Read Philippians 4:1-5. Paul writes a lot of short commands in this final chapter. As you read, pay attention to the many things Paul commands the church to do.

- [ ] Open your notebook to a new page and label it Philippians 4:1-5 at the top.

- [ ] Doodle the outline of a church. Make it really big, taking up your whole notebook page because we will doodle inside it. Now, inside the church, doodle two grouchy looking women who are arguing with each other. Don't draw them too big. (Be sure to leave enough space for writing and more doodles.) These two ladies are the ones mentioned here, Euodia and Syntyche. Though Paul doesn't say, it is fair to assume that their disagreement was a big deal since Paul is calling them out in front of everyone. (I like to think they were arguing about whose name was the worst!)

PHILIPPIANS 4:1-5

☐ Label Euodia and Syntyche, and then reread verses 2 and 3. Write down what you learn about them from these verses. (You might even want to use the description as a kind of border around them.)

☐ So, while Paul is encouraging these two Christian women to get along, what is he encouraging the rest of the church to do? Inside your church, draw a small crowd of people. (Again, leave enough room to write.)

☐ Reread verses 1-5 and write down everything Paul says about the church people - how he describes them and what he commands them to do. For example, from verse 1 you could write "loved," "my joy and crown," and "stand firm." Of course, have fun with fonts and doodles where you can!

☐ Look over your notebook page. What do you notice? Do you think Paul's descriptions and commands to the church also apply to Euodia and Syntyche? Do you think if you were in a disagreement with someone it would be easy to rejoice (verse 4) or be reasonable (or gentle) as Paul says (in verse 5)? Do you think it was easy for Euodia to think of Syntyche as "beloved" or for Syntyche to see Euodia as Paul's "joy and crown"? Why or why not?

☐ What about you? Is there another Christian you often disagree with? How can the example of Euodia and Syntyche help you? How can Paul's description and commands change your perspective? Journal your ideas.

PHILIPPIANS 4:1-5

Going Deeper: Did you notice Paul's command to the Philippians to "help these women" get along? What else does the Bible say about quarreling and being a peacemaker? Quite a lot, actually! Read these verses from Proverbs for a Biblical perspective on the sin that so easily catches so many of us. If you find that you really struggle with being argumentative, try memorizing one (or more) of these verses. With God's Word and the Holy Spirit in your heart, you can overcome temptation.

I'M RIGHT!!

YOU ARE SO WRONG!!

- *Proverbs 12:20
- *Proverbs 13:10
- *Proverbs 15:18
- *Proverbs 17:14
- *Proverbs 26:20

PHILIPPIANS 4:6-9

☐ Begin your time in prayer. Is there anything troubling you or causing you to worry? If so, tell God about it, asking Him to provide what you need in the situation. Ask God to give you His peace and His wisdom.

☐ Read Philippians 4:6-9. Just a few short verses! As you read, pay attention to all that Paul is commanding the Philippians.

Philippians 4:6-9

☐ Open your notebook to a fresh page and label it Philippians 4:6-9.

When you read the passage, did you notice Paul's command "do not be anxious"? We might not use the word "anxious" to describe how we feel, but what Paul is telling the Christians in Philippi is, "Don't worry!"

Let's remember Paul's circumstances - he is chained to a Roman guard each and every day, unable to freely travel or start new churches. He could only visit friends if they came to see him. He is not really able to work, but needed food, clothes, and a place to live. All through this, Paul is awaiting a trial before Caesar, a man who thinks of himself as some kind of god. Caesar will decide if Paul should be executed for spreading Christianity in his empire. Do you think Paul has anything to worry about?

And what about the Philippians? Let's not forget about them. Their pastor is in prison, their good friend Epaphroditus just nearly died doing them a favor, and they are persecuted and opposed by family, neighbors, and the government for following this "crazy religion" started by a Jewish rabbi, Jesus. Maybe they've even already seen some of their Christian friends killed for following Christ. Do you think THEY have things to worry about?

The answer is, of course they do! Paul and the Philippians had all kinds of things to worry about! Let's not forget that when we read Paul's words "Do not be anxious about anything." In fact, it's likely that the reason Paul wrote "do not worry" is because the Philippians had so many things to worry about!

PHILIPPIANS 4:6-9

Thankfully, God has not left us on our own to figure out how to obey Him. When He tells us "do not be anxious" He lovingly guides us to do what He says. We will take a closer look at the passage to find out how we can do that, but let's take a closer look at our own hearts first.

☐ In your notebook you are going to draw four rectangles or boxes. Label the first rectangle "My Top 3 Worries." Maybe you have more than three - that's okay. If you have less than three that's okay too. Write down in the box whatever is in your heart that makes you anxious.

— MY TOP THREE WORRIES...FEARS...CONCERNS....—

☐ Draw your next box and label it "My Way of Dealing with My Worries." In this box, think about what you do when you start feeling worried. Do you talk to someone? Distract yourself with screen time? Eat? Hide under the covers? You might also journal off to the side how you feel - what does worry feel like to you? How would you describe it?

— MY WAY OF DEALING WITH MY WORRIES —   how I feel when I worry

PHILIPPIANS 4:6-9

☐ Hopefully you've done a good job of taking an honest look at your own heart. But we can't stop there! Now we need to apply what the Bible says to our fears and worries. Draw your third box and label it "Paul's Prescription for Worry." (Remembering, of course, that what Paul says we should do is God's Word to you!) Reread verses 6, 8, and 9 to fill in your box with God's commands to us. (There are three.)

―――― PAUL'S PRESCRIPTION FOR WORRY ――――

☐ Did you find the three commands? Here's help if you need it. The first (from verse 6) - let God know what you need through prayer. The second (verse 8) - think about things that are true, honorable, just, pure, lovely, commendable, excellent, and praiseworthy. And the last command (from verse 9) - imitate godly living you see in other believers.

How rarely we think to do these things when we are stressed out, worried, or feeling fearful! In my own life I do just about everything *but* those three things. Yet when I do, God is faithful! Our own hearts try to find ways to overcome our anxieties. The world tells us there are "healthy" and "unhealthy" ways to dealing with stress. But God's Word is the only trustworthy, spiritual truth that can truly free us from anxiety.

☐ Draw your fourth and final box. Title it "What God Promises He Will Do."

PHILIPPIANS 4:6-9

☐ This is the really beautiful part, friends! Reread verses 7 and 9. What does God promise to His children who come to Him in prayer with their worries? What does God say He will do for those who think on good things instead of all the "what-ifs" of life? Fill in your fourth box.

--- GOD'S PROMISES FOR OUR WORRY ---

Isn't that AMAZING? When we follow God's commands, we can experience God's peace (verse 7) and God's very presence (verse 9).

☐ If you want, you can draw another heart out to the side of your fourth box. How does the peace of God feel? How is that different than how you feel when you worry? What is it like to have the God of Peace with you? What will you do differently the next time you feel anxious, scared, or worried? Journal your thoughts.

❓ Are you sitting here thinking, "Well, this is great and all, but I've *never* had God's peace in my heart." God's promises are for His children, so if you have truly never experienced the peace of God please turn to page 77 to read about the Gospel. You will never experience peace *from* God until you have peace *with* God. Peace with God comes when we repent of our sin and trust God to save us. (Romans 5:1) Please seek out a trusted Christian friend to answer questions you have about salvation. Do not delay!

PHILIPPIANS 4:6-9

➡️ **Going Deeper**: Want to know more about what God's Word teaches us about worry and having peace? Read some or all of these verses on the peace of God. May you be comforted! God is peace, and true peace comes from God alone.

- *Matthew 6:25-34
- *John 16:33
- *Colossians 3:15
- *John 14:27
- *Ephesians 2:13-14
- *2 Thessalonians 3:16

➡️ **Going Deeper**: In verse 8, Paul gives us the command to fill our mind with thoughts that are good. Why is this so important? All through Scripture we are told to keep watch over our thoughts because God knows that whatever fills your mind (and heart) will guide you to be the person you become. If you want to live right, you must first think right.

☐ On a page in your journal, list out in a column all the words Paul uses to describe our thoughts in verse 8. In a column next to the first one, write down the opposite of each word. Which column better describes your thoughts?

☐ What feeds your mind? There are so many sources! Conversations with friends, TV, music, books, the internet, games...If you put garbage in, you will not be able to think about things that are excellent or lovely no matter how hard you try. Feed your mind truth from God's Word.

❗ Beware of your own heart! - we (and the world) say "lovely," awesome," and "excellent." God says "false," "trash," and "despicable." Learn God's Word to know God's ways!

68

Overheard in an Orchard

Said the Robin to the Sparrow
"I would really like to know
Why these anxious human beings
Rush about and worry so."

Said the Sparrow to the Robin,
"Friend, I think that it must be
that they have no heavenly Father
as cares for you and me."

~Elizabeth Cheney

> ## HEBREWS 11:32-40
>
> And what more shall I say? For time would fail me to tell of Gideon, Barak, Samson, Jephthah, of David and Samuel and the prophets - who through faith
> conquered kingdoms,
> enforced justice,
> obtained promises,
> stopped the mouths of lions,
> quenched the power of fire,
> escaped the edge of the sword,
> were made strong out of weakness,
> became mighty in war,
> put foreign armies to flight.
> Women received back their dead by resurrection.
>
> Some were tortured, refusing to accept release,
> so that they might rise again to a better life.
> Others suffered mocking and flogging,
> and even chains and imprisonment.
> They were stoned,
> they were sawn in two,
> they were killed with the sword.
> They went about in skins of sheep and goats,
> destitute, afflicted, mistreated -
> of whom the world was not worthy -
> wandering about in deserts and mountains,
> and in dens and caves of the earth.
>
> And all these, though commended through their faith, did not receive what was promised, since God had provided something better for us, that apart from us they should not be made perfect.

PHILIPPIANS 4:10-23

- [ ] Begin your time in prayer. In 1 Chronicles 16:11 we are told to "Seek the Lord and His strength. Seek His presence continually!" Pray, asking God that as you seek Him through this Bible study that He will make His presence known to you. Ask God to help you know Him more.

- [ ] We are coming to the end of Philippians! Open your notebook to a new page. Label it Philippians 4:10-23.

- [ ] Before you read the passage for today, think about contentment. What does it mean to be content? Have you ever felt it? What does discontent look like? Use a dictionary to add to your ideas if you like. Journal your thoughts.

DISCONTENT xXx

CONTENT

- [ ] Now Read Philippians 4:10-23. Paul is thanking the Philippians for joining him in the work of spreading the gospel. As you read, pay attention to Paul's attitude. How would you describe Paul from this passage?

- [ ] In your notebook, doodle Paul. Reread the passage and write down everything you learn about Paul from these verses, focusing especially on his attitude of contentment. You might even want to doodle a few speech bubbles of things he says. When could he be content? How does he feel towards the Philippians? Does this add to his contentment? What helped him be content?

I have learned the secret of being content

Philippians 4:10-23

☐ Reread verses 13 and 19. What did Paul believe about God that helped him be content? Be sure to add this to your notebook.

➡️ **Going Deeper**: You will really be amazed by how God worked in Paul's life if you know more about the circumstances Paul lived through. When Paul says he *learned* to be content in **any** and **every** situation, he encourages us that we too can learn to be content in the circumstances God gives us. Read 1 Corinthians 4:11-13, 2 Corinthians 6:4-5, and 2 Corinthians 11:24-28. Add what you learn about Paul's "any and every situation" to your notebook.

☐ Turn to a fresh page in your notebook. Doodle yourself in the center. Write words and phrases around your doodle that describe your circumstances. What words or phrases would you use to describe your attitude or beliefs towards your circumstances? How does your page compare to your Paul page? How would you like to change? Take some time to pray about your heart and where you are these days.

➡️ **Going Deeper**: Take some time to reflect more on where you are in the journey of learning contentment. Where have you learned contentment? Where do you still struggle? How can knowing (and believing) that God will strengthen you (verse 13) and supply your needs (verse 19) apply to your circumstances? How do these truths change your perspective? Journal your thoughts.

Philippians 4:10-23

? What does Paul mean when he says in verse 13 that he can do everything through Christ? Does he mean that if I'm a Christian that I will have powers like a superhero? Or that I can pass a test I haven't studied for? Does it mean that if I sincerely pray about it, I can do anything I ask God to help me do?

Sadly, this verse is one that is most often quoted from the Bible but probably most often misused. Too many people think Paul means that "through Christ" they can achieve their wildest dreams. I remember shouting it at my friend as she tried to climb a rope at summer camp. I thought if she just believed enough, that God would give her the arm strength to succeed. When she didn't I thought to myself that she probably just needed more faith. Oops.

So if Paul didn't mean to say that we can literally do *everything* through Christ, what did he mean?

As with any verse, context is so important! Key to understanding Paul's meaning is noticing that he writes verse 13 while talking about how he's content whatever the circumstance. I think the NIV Bible captures his meaning best by translating, "I can do all this through Christ who gives me strength."

So whether Paul was hungry or full, needy or living in plenty, he was content - he could do it! - because Christ gave him the strength he needed.

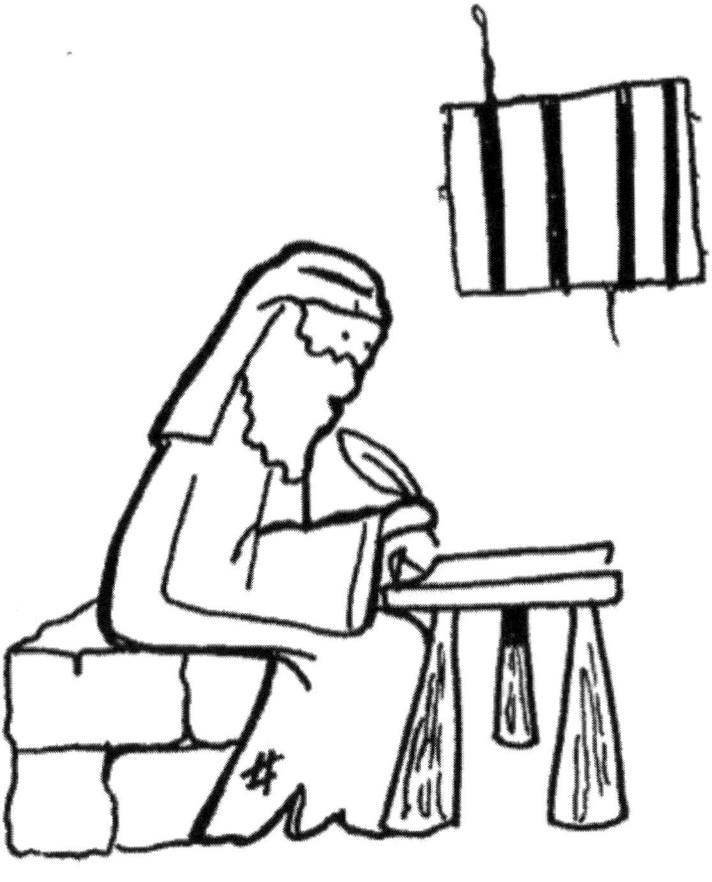

Wait! I'm Not Ready to Be Done With Philippians!

If that's how you feel, here's some ideas to make your time in Philippians last a little longer.

*Go through your notebook looking for any places you could add more doodles, color, or additional thoughts. (Use the Doodle Library on the following pages for inspiration.)

*Is there any part of the study you skipped over? Go back and do it now.

*If someone asked you about Philippians, could you tell them what it's about?

*Go back through your notebook and reflect on your learning. What stands out to you the most? How did God use this study to challenge you, speak to you, or change you?

*Using a concordance or an online tool like Biblegateway.com, look up one (or more) of the words repeated in Philippians - "joy," "rejoice," or "gospel." What do other parts of Scripture tell you about joy, rejoicing, or the gospel?

*Watch the "Read Scripture: Philippians" video on YouTube or via the Read Scripture app. It's a great summary!

*Memorize key verses from Philippians. There are so many to choose from and several are really short, making them easy to memorize. Here are a few suggestions, but the best ones to memorize are the ones that speak to you the most.
- Philippians 1:6
- Philippians 1:21
- Philippians 2:3
- Philippians 3:8
- Philippians 4:4
- Philippians 4:6-7

the end

What is the Gospel?

GOD RULES
GENESIS 1:1, ISAIAH 33:22, COLOSSIANS 1:16

God is the Creator of the entire world. He is the holy, righteous, sovereign King. He alone determines what is right and wrong. He created men and women to know Him, to walk with Him, and to obey Him.

WE SINNED
ISAIAH 53:6, ROMANS 3:10-12; ROMANS 6:23

Sadly, we don't want to obey God. We want to go our own way and decide for ourselves what is best. That's sin. We thought we could make ourselves happy without God. Instead, we became lost. Like confused sheep in the dark of night we suddenly could not find our way. Because of sin, our relationship with God is broken. Sin keeps us from knowing God. The punishment for our sin is death.

GOD RESCUES
ISAIAH 53:5, JOHN 3:16, ROMANS 3:23-24, ROMANS 5:8

Our sin has destroyed our relationship with God. Our own hearts are twisted, and we cannot do what is right. Like a drowning man who is unable to save himself, we need a rescue. In love, God sent His Son Jesus who lived a perfect, sinless life to die in our place. After His death on the cross, He was resurrected as proof that our debt had been paid.

WE BELIEVE
ACTS 16:31, ROMANS 10:9-10, EPHESIANS 2:8-9, COLOSSIANS 1:13-14

We need to turn away from our sin and turn to God, receiving His gift of salvation. By believing that Jesus has paid for your sin, you are rescued from darkness. Your sins are forgiven, and you are brought into God's family. You will live in heaven with God forever.

WE LIVE
1 PETER 1:13-16, 1 PETER 2:1-3, 1 JOHN 3:10

We know we deserved to die, but God has given us life. To show God our love and thanks for all He has done, we live holy lives, obedient to His commands. We learn to walk in His ways through prayer, reading the Bible, worshipping Him at church, and telling others about Him.

Doodle Library

inspiration to get your artsy inside to the outside

- arrows
- flourishes
- borders
- banners
- people
- swords & crowns
- books & letters
- places
- and more!

-HOW TO DOODLE PAUL-

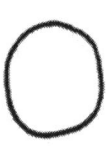

1 BEGIN BY DRAWING A CIRCLE FOR HIS HEAD

2 DRAW TWO SLIGHTLY ARCHED LINES FOR HIS BODY.

5 ERASE FACE LINES UNDER THE BEARD. ADD EYES.

6 DRAW ARMS AND SIMPLE HANDS. ADD ON HIS TURBAN.

-a step by step guide-

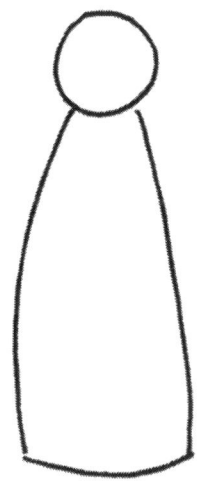

3 Close the bowling pin body with a slightly arched line connecting the sides.

4 Doodle a beard

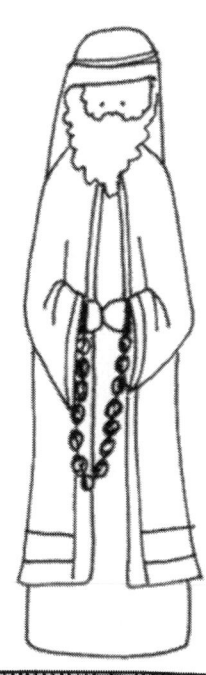

You will improve with practice and develop your own style too. As you improve, you can add other details like chains or multiple layers of clothing. Experiment with other expressions and positions too!

82

83

84

gospel

PRESS ON !!

JAIL

world
CHRIST
FAITH

pray

PAUL
to the saints
in Philippi

thank you

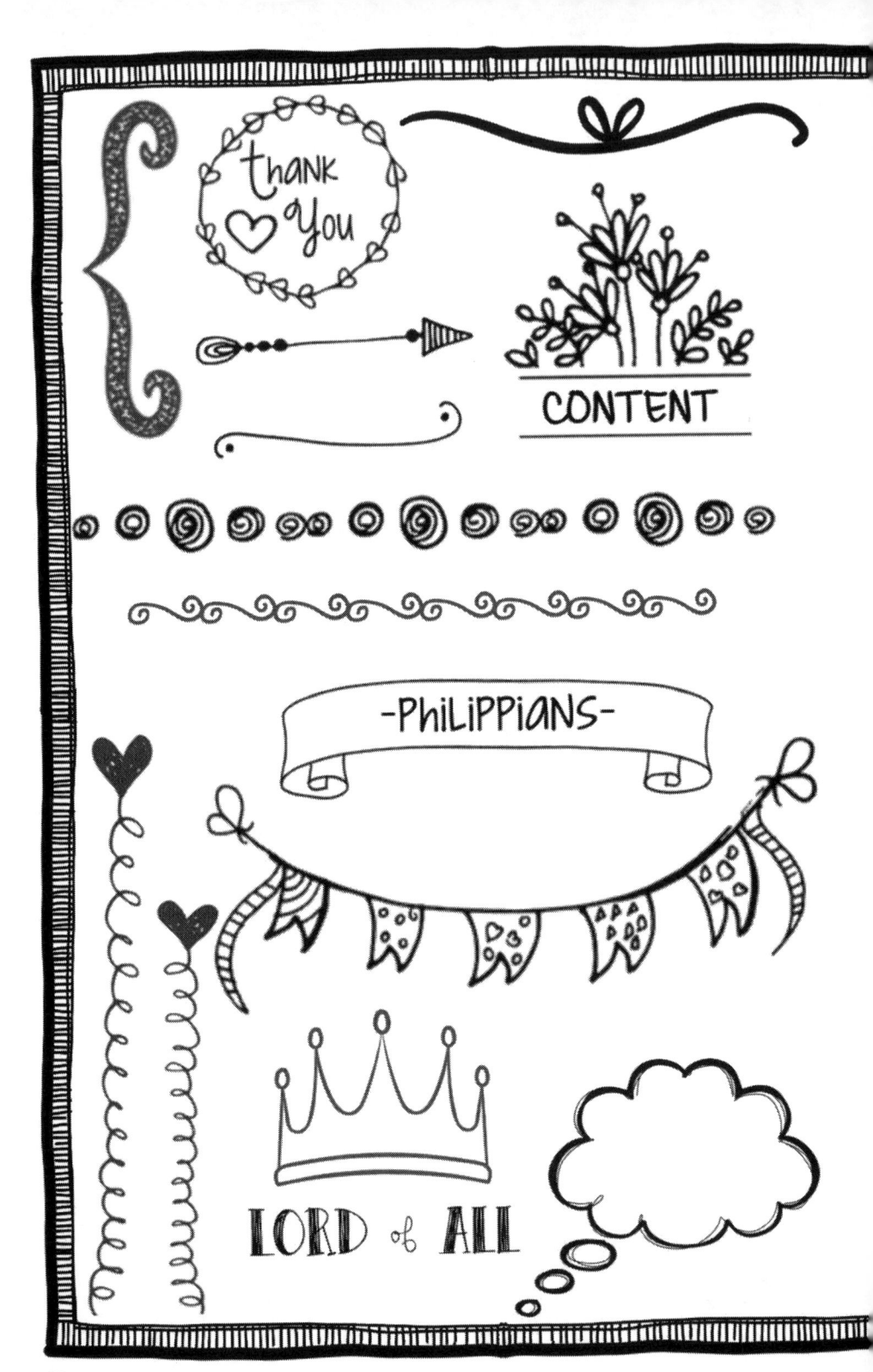

CONTENT

-Philippians-

LORD of ALL

I WILL FOLLOW

rejoice

THANK YOU!

PROCLAIM
without fear

HEAVEN BOUND

PAUL

SHINING LIKE STARS IN THE SKY

PHILIPPIANS

grace AND PEACE

timothy

let this mind be in you

♡ humility ♡

which is yours in Christ Jesus

"I have learned the secret of being content"

GOD OPPOSES THE **PROUD** BUT GIVES GRACE TO THE *humble*

I ONE LORD
ONE FAITH
ONE BAPTISM
ONE GOD
and
FATHER of ALL

WORTHY of the GOSPEL

Same mind. Same love.
—UNITED—
One Spirit. One Purpose.
(Verse 2)

Epaphroditus

DISCONTENT
xxx

YOU ARE SO WRONG!!

PRESS ON...

A Note from the Author

Hello, friend - You did it! You made it to the end of the book!

I hope that you enjoyed your time of reading, studying, and doodling your way through the book of Philippians. I have prayed that God has used this study to teach you more about God, inspire you to follow Jesus more closely, and to encourage you in your faith.

I would love to hear from you! If you have any lingering questions, comments about the study, or just want to share your thoughts about your walk of faith, please email me at bibleanddoodle@gmail.com.

> Now may the God of peace
> who brought again from the dead our Lord Jesus...
> equip you with everything good that you may do his will,
> working in us that which is pleasing in his sight,
> through Jesus Christ,
> to whom be glory forever and ever. Amen.

With great joy & for God's glory,
Kristen

ENDNOTES

1. Merida, Tony and Francis Chan. *Christ Centered Exposition: Exalting Jesus in Philippians.* B&H Publishing Group, 2016.
2. Chandler, Matt and Jared Wilson. *To Live is Christ to Die is Gain.* David C. Cook, 2014.
3. Lawson, Steven J. *Philippians for You.* The Good Book Company, 2017.
4. "Grace." *International Standard Bible Encyclopedia.* www.blueletterbible.org/search/Dictionary/viewTopic.cfm?topic=IT0003910. Accessed April 22, 2017.
5. Merida, Tony and Francis Chan.
6. Ibid.
7. Qureshi, Nabeel. *Seeking Allah, Finding Jesus.* Zondervan, 2014.
8. Greear, J.D. *Gospel: Recovering the Power that Made Christianity Revolutionary.* B&H Publishing Group, 2011.
9. Belz, Mindy. *They Say We Are Infidels: On the Run from ISIS with Persecuted Christians in the Middle East.* Tyndale Momentum, 2016.
10. Lawson, Steven J.
11. Qureshi, Nabeel. *No God But One: Allah or Jesus? : A Former Muslim Investigates the Evidence for Islam and Christianity.* Zondervan, 2016.
12. Helland, Pete. "The Making of a Nobody." 7 May 2017, Grace Bible Church, New Whiteland, IN. Sermon.
13. Foxe, John. *Foxe's Book of Martyrs.* Thomas Nelson, Inc., 2000.
14. Lifton, Bryan M. *Early Christian Martyr Stories: An Evangelical Introduction with New Translations.* Baker Academic, 2014.
15. Klumpenhower, Jack. *Show Them Jesus.* New Growth Press, 2014.
16. Lifton, Bryan M.
17. "Nate Saint." *MAF Mission Aviation Fellowship.* www.maf.org/about/history/nate-saint. Accessed September 6, 2017.

Made in the USA
Lexington, KY
04 June 2018